On Knowing Oneself Too Well

On Knowing Oneself Too Well

●●●●●●●●●●●●●●●●●●●●●●●●●●●●●

SELECTED POEMS OF
ISHIKAWA TAKUBOKU

Translated by Tamae K. Prindle

SYLLABIC PRESS 2010

© 2010 Syllabic Press
All rights reserved. Published 2010
Printed in the United States of America

ISBN 978-0-615-34562-8

Syllabic Press
200 E. Joppa Road, Suite L-101
Towson, MD 21286
syllabicpress@gmail.com

Publication of this book was supported by
a grant from the Maryland State Arts Council.

Library of Congress Card No. 2010900062

Contents

Acknowledgments — vii
Introduction — ix

"Let us sing" — 3
An Aeroplane — 3
To a Crab — 4
A LOVE SONG TO MYSELF — 5
I Will Go Alone — 25
To My Sister — 26
A White Face — 29
SMOKE (1) — 30
A Feeble Thought — 38
SMOKE (2) — 39
You, Flower — 47
IN RESPONSE TO A PLEASANT AUTUMN WIND — 48
The Illusion of Cherry Blossoms — 51
A Crossroad — 53
The Moon and the Gong — 55
To a Takuboku Bird — 56
August — 57
A Willow Leaf — 58
After an Endless Discussion — 59
An Epitaph — 60
A Fist — 62
Don't Wake Up — 63
UNFORGETTABLE PEOPLE (1) — 64
An Old Man — 77
UNFORGETTABLE PEOPLE (2) — 78
WHEN I TAKE MY GLOVES OFF — 81

No Title (1)	97
SAD TOYS	99
No Title (2)	124
In a Wagon	126
An Afternoon in My Study	127
Home	128

Acknowledgments

I am grateful to Professor John Ehrstine at the Washington State University (WSU) English Department who suggested that I translate Japanese poems into English. I am also deeply indebted to Professor Hack Chin Kim at WSU who closely supervised my translation. Robert Schreur kindly brought the book to publication for Syllabic Press.

The poems translated in this volume come principally from the two-volume collection *Ishikawa Takuboku-shū,* edited by Tsunatake Furuya (Shinchō Bunko, 1950).

T.K.P.

Introduction

ISHIKAWA TAKUBOKU was born into a well-educated Buddhist monk's family on October 27, 1885 in Hinoto Village in northern Japan. (His birthdate was officially recorded as February 20, 1886 in the village census, causing discrepancies about his age at the time of his death.) The third of four children, but the only son, his given name was Hajime, meaning "first one." According to a sister's memoir, he was very much his mother and father's favorite. He distinguished himself at school and took an early interest in literature. At sixteen he was caught cheating on a mathematics exam and left school, living briefly in Tokyo. He soon gained recognition from important literary figures of the day for his essays, fiction, and poetry, written in both traditional forms and the longer shintaishi ("new-style") form, influenced by Western verse.

At eighteen he was given the pen-name Takuboku, meaning "woodpecker," by the poet Yasano Tekkan. At nineteen he married his childhood sweetheart, Setsu Hariai. At this time his father was discharged from his position as temple priest, and Takuboku became responsible for supporting his family, which expanded with the birth of his daughter, Kyoko, when he was twenty-one. He found work as a substitute teacher but was fired after organizing a student strike against the school principal. His family was forced to live apart — his mother returned to their hometown, his wife and daughter went to live with his wife's family, and Takuboku moved to the far northern city of Hakodate to work as an editor, until he was forced to leave after a major portion of the city was destroyed in a fire.

He then found work in various cities as a proof-reader, reporter, and editor. Occasionally able to reunite his family, he was frequently forced by poverty to separate again, often surviving solely on small loans and gifts from friends. He became deeply interested in socialism and was remarkably prolific, writing nine novels and nearly a thousand poems in one year, sometimes composing fifty or more poems in a single night.

At age twenty-two he fell in love with a geisha, Koyakko, whom he names in several poems. At twenty-four his son, Shinichi, was born, dying twenty-three days later. A month afterward his first volume of tanka poems, *A Handful of Sand,* was published. Takuboku spent the advance he received for the book to pay for his son's funeral.

In this volume (consisting of the seven tanka-sequences in the present collection, exclusive of SAD TOYS), Takuboku followed the innovative practice of his contemporary Toki Aiki in presenting tanka (traditionally five units of 5, 7, 5, 7, and 7 syllables) in three lines of variable length. In their subject-matter, diction, and purpose, the poems brought a frank immediacy and striking modernity to this twelve-century-old poetic form.

Soon after the book's publication, Takuboku was diagnosed with tuberculosis and began a series of hospitalizations, ending in his death on April 12, 1912 at age twenty-six. His mother had died a month previously of tuberculosis, and a year later his wife died of the disease. Takuboku's second volume of tanka, *Sad Toys,* was published posthumously two months after his death.

On Knowing Oneself Too Well

"Let us sing"

Let us sing
When, worn-out by incessant battle, joints of our limbs ache,
When a deep woe visits us,
When our child suffers in deathbed,
When we see a beggar who resembles our mother,
When we have exhausted our soul in love—
Let us sing at those moments,
Gazing into a silent sky,
O my starved comrades.

An Aeroplane

Look, today again,
At the aeroplane high in the blue sky.

A page boy
On one of his few Sundays off
In a house alone with his consumptive mother,
The fatigue of his eyes from the busy solitary study of a self-tutorial text-book . . .

Look, today again,
At the aeroplane high in the blue sky.

To a Crab

You, clever crab on this eastern seashore,
Hiding in a hole at high tide,
Emerging from it at low tide,
Always walking sideways—
Do you know or don't you know
That a tired child saunters by,
Swept by a fatal tide,
Led by a shimmering light smaller than your eyes?

A Love Song to Myself

On the white sand of an eastern islet,
Wet with tears,
I play with a crab.

> My memory lingers on the person
> Who showed me a handful of sand,
> His cheeks wet with tears.

I left my home
To cry for several days
Facing the ocean.

> The indifference of lifeless sand—
> Quickly it falls
> Through the gap in my clenched fingers.

The ball of wet sand
Made by my tears—
Are my tears heavy then?

I wrote the symbol LARGE on the sand
A hundred odd times
And returned home, deciding not to die.

    It is a sad habit
    To linger in bed in the morning,
    But scold me not, my mother.

I spit on a hunk of soil
And form my mother's crying face—
Oh, how dreary!

    I sit in a murky room;
    Father and Mother with canes
    Emerge from within the wall.

Carrying my mother on my back in jest
I failed to walk as many as three steps,
Weeping over her being so light.

    Though my friends laugh at my habit
    Of wandering out of the house
    And wandering into the house . . .

Like my father in our village,
I cough also—
The fear of consumption!

    I slept, exhausted,
    Feeling my soul
    Being sucked into a dark hole.

Were there a pleasant job for me to try
I would complete it
Before I died.

    I curl myself up
    In a corner of a crowded train—
    Night after night I grow more endearing to myself!

The lonely feeling
Of slipping out of Asakura's evening crowd—◆
After being part of it.

    I cut the ear off my pet-dog—
    Damn!
    Is this what I do when I'm tired?

◆ A large shopping district in Tokyo.

In front of a mirror,
I try all sorts of facial expressions
When I am tired of crying.

    Tears, tears,
    How strange!
    When I wash them, I feel playful.

Hearing my mother's stupefied utterance,
I realize
That I had been striking a rice-bowl with my chopsticks.

    On my blank face
    As I lay on the grass
    A bird pooped, playing in the air.

The downward growth
Of my beard is provoking;
It makes me resemble the man I have been hating lately.

    I found myself
    Pressing my ear against a large tree
    As I peeled the hard bark for half a day.

Shall I die for such a thing?
Shall I live for such a thing?
An endless controversy.

> In the rare tranquility of my mind
> The chimes of the clock
> Strike my ears pleasantly.

Suddenly frightened
Into immobility,
I slowly felt for my belly-button.

> I climbed up to the summit of a mountain
> And came down waving my hat
> For no reason.

I will break one flowerpot in each fit of anger—
Then I shall have nine-hundred-and-ninety-nine pots broken
When I die.

> The resentful expression of the short man
> Whom I see in the train everyday
> Began bothering me lately.

✦ An allusion to the Japanese saying, "Thunder steals your belly-button."

In front of a mirror shop
I was suddenly struck:
What a wreck I am!

> I was, somehow, tempted to ride on a train,
> But found nowhere to go
> When I got off.

I once entered an empty house
And smoked a cigarette
Just to be alone and feel miserable.

> It's been three months
> Since I became a man
> Who would wander around when he is lonely.

I wish to experience the sort of love
That compels the dipping of my burning face
In softly piled snow.

> Pitiable is a man
> Who is fed up
> With his ever-craving ego.

Stretching my arms and my legs
Out across a room,
I get up slowly.

> As if waking from a hundred-years' slumber,
> I wish I could yawn
> Free of cares.

Folding my arms,
I have come to think lately
That I am ready to challenge any unconquerable enemy.

> I met a man who is said to be "extraordinary"—
> His hands were white
> Yet large.

Generously,
I felt like praising somebody—
No matter how forlorn my ego is.

> The rain
> Makes my family feel low—
> Rain, go away!

Isn't there a way
Of ending life
As if leaping from a high place?

> The other day
> The grudge that had secretly lodged in my mind
> Made me laugh.

I resent flattery—
It is pitiful
To know oneself too well.

> The jest of knocking on a stranger's door at night
> Only to run swiftly away—
> I'm nostalgic for my younger days.

The ennui
After pretending to be somebody—
What shall I compare it to?

> His large body was hateful
> When I was obliged to say something
> In front of it.

I borrowed some money from the man
Who understands me to be a man
Of no practical use.

    I hear flute music in the distance—
    Is it because my head hangs down
    That my tears fall?

I envy the frivolity of the man
Who likes this
As much as that.

    Death:
    It seems the same as taking some medicine—
    Since my heart aches so.

On the road-side, a dog gave a long yawn;
I did the same
In envy.

    The serious expression of a child
    Beating a dog with a bamboo stick—
    I define that as beautiful.

◆ A bamboo stick traditionally symbolizes "innocence" or "ignorance."

"The pleasant groaning of a dynamo"—
How sad it is
To say such a thing!

    The pale fatigue
    In my facetious friend's dead face—
    It remains vivid in my memory.

I worked for an inconstant man
And felt
Thoroughly disgusted with this world.

    Leaping like a dragon into an empty sky
    The smoke disappears—
    A sight which never bores me.

A pleasant fatigue,
The fatigue
After breathless toil.

    Stopping the movement of my chopsticks, I suddenly realize
    That I'm finally
    Adjusted to a normal life.

Early in the morning
I read what seems like a love-letter from my sister—
She has passed marriageable age.

    I experienced a weight
    Similar to
    A soaked-up sponge.

A bestial face
Opened and closed its mouth—
This is how I saw the man talk.

    It was one of the passengers
    On that boat and on that voyage
    Who could not bring himself to die.

The cookie dish in front of me—
I wish to chew it with a crunchy sound.
How frustrating!

    The ever-laughing man—
    When he dies
    The world will be a little more monotonous.

I don't know why
But I feel like running till I am breathless on the plains,
Or some such place.

    I will travel
    In a new suit—
    Another year has passed in this thought.

I ceremoniously turn off the light
And collect my thoughts
On some inconsequential matter.

    At the summit of Asakusa Ryōunkaku ◆
    I folded my arms,
    According to a long entry in my diary.

Rushing out of my house,
I found warmth in the sunlight;
So, I breathed heartily.

    Wondering what they are doing,
    I stare with a severe face
    At the group that uses pickaxes.

◆ A twelve-story building in Tokyo, erected in 1890. One of the first buildings to have an elevator, it was partially destroyed by an earthquake in 1932 and later dismantled.

A giant spirit came—
As I walk
I feel the power stored in my stomach.

    To cry alone,
    I came and lay down—
    Ah, the comfort of inn mattresses.

The smell of fresh ink—
When the bottle is uncapped,
It penetrates to my empty stomach.

    Misery is
    When I shrink in a cold bed
    And bear the thirst in my throat.

Whoever made me bow
Even once—
I pray they all may die.

    Two of my buddies,
    One has died and the other
    Took to bed after getting out of jail.

Despite his excessive talent,
Alas, my friend suffers
From his wife.

> I confessed all to him
> And felt as though I was taken advantage of
> When we parted.

Watching a dull cloudy sky,
Oh, I felt like
Killing somebody.

> The pensive complaint
> Of a fellow of average intelligence
> Is pitiable.

A man of no merit
Visited and went away proudly—
How humiliating!

> No matter how hard I work
> My life remains poor—
> I stare at my hands in wonder.

Just as I crave alcohol
On some days,
I crave money today.

> With no trouble
> I grow fat pleasantly—
> This wastefulness of my days.

To my conceited friend
I give a nod of consent
In the spirit of doing him a favor.

> At the end of a sad dream one morning
> The smell of cooked bean-paste soup ◆
> Came to my nose.

Knock knock, the sound of a stone being cut in a field
Remained in my ears
Till I entered the house.

> I have a kind of cliff in my head
> From which the soil keeps eroding
> Day after day.

◆ Misoshiru, bean-paste soup, is served for breakfast in traditional Japanese homes.

Like a telephone ringing in the distance
My ears ring again
On this sad day.

> When I desperately wish to die
> I hide myself in a bathroom
> And make menacing faces.

Japanese people look unbearably ignoble today.
I will therefore
Stay at home.

> I will sleep the whole day
> When a holiday comes—
> That has been my wish for three years.

The feeling of a certain day—
I liken it to
Oven-hot bread.

> One day
> I renewed the paper on my shōji-screens; *
> I was consoled for that day.

---

* Sliding doors made of wooden frames with checkered panes of white paper.

Motionless,
I observe the sponge
Dried hard from black or red ink.

> This evening
> I feel like writing a letter so long
> It would make anybody miss me.

Fed up with my desk-lamp,
For three days
I have enjoyed candlelight.

> Words which nobody uses—
> It suddenly struck me today:
> Is it possible that they are known only to myself?

In search of a fresh frame of mind
I rambled streets again
Whose names I do not know.

> On the day when all my friends seem greater than I,
> I buy some flowers
> And enjoy my wife's company at home.

I want a place to play till morning—
As the thought of home
Freezes me.

    How sad it is that everybody has his own home—
    As though entering a grave,
    I go home and retire.

When scolded,
Children burst into tears—
I itch to take their place.

    My hopeless mind
    Which does not consider a theft to be wicked—
    I have no shelter to hide myself.

On a garden stone
I smashed a clock—
I'm nostalgic for the anger I once had.

    I blush with resentment—
    Its pointlessness grieves me
    The next day.

You silly irritated soul,
Come, come!
Let us yawn for awhile.

> A woman
> Who strives not to argue with me—
> How pathetic to see her!

The cowardice
Of Japanese women—
I cursed it on a rainy day in autumn.

> All my thoughts
> Seem to result from my poverty—
> Oh, the autumn wind blows.

The autumn wind—
From today on
I will never speak to that fat man.

> Today I luckily have spirit
> Equal to
> Walking a straight endless road.

I will never forget the days
I have lived
Without a thought, though occupied.

> I laugh off money problems.
> But soon
> I begin bitching about them again.

Whoever may shoot me
With a gun:
I am ready to die as Itō did. ◆

> Forcibly
> Prime Minister Katsura grabbed my arm— ◆◆
> My dream left me there at two o' clock one
>   autumn night.

◆ Hirobumi Itō was Japan's first Prime Minister. An unpopular aristrocrat, he was assassinated in Manchuria in 1909.

◆◆ Katsura Tarō, a former army general, served three terms as Japan's Prime Minister.

I Will Go Alone

The day is done.
>*(A miserable life)*

Into the forest of illusion
Now I enter alone.
All the sounds are muted;
>*(Oh, my life)*

The forest of memory showered by a delicate melody.
>*(The thought of night,
>the thought of life)*

The romance is achieved.
>*(The life of fantasy)*

Into the self-oblivious forest
Now I enter alone.
The perfume of poppies slackens;
>*(Oh, my life)*

The forest where a thin green mist of my breath wavers.
>*(The smell of night,
>the smell of love)*

The romance is destroyed.
>*(The life of woe)*

Into the forest of prayer
Now I enter alone.
The image of her face as I pray;
>*(Oh, my life)*

The forest of love refreshed by a celestial Muse.
>*(The prayer of night,
>the prayer of life)*

The moon shines.
    (*A colorful life*)
Into the forest of illusion
Now I enter alone.
The soft moonlight in the forest
    (*Oh, my life*)
Illuminates the golden flower banks of my hometown.
    (*The life of night,
      Oh, my life*)

To My Sister

To Takaka Horiai

Was a frigid wind blowing? In September
The smell of young, green leaves purifies
My dreams in this lonely hut.
After breakfast in my room,
In the middle of a pleasant tea,
My green incense burner broke
And the wind carried the fresh air.
Following suit
I cleaned my hands and burned some incense.
Wondering what the smell was from,
My sister, you calmly smiled at me.

Against the low gray mask of a city sky
On the southern side of a cedar temple,

You pointed at the winging white pigeons
On the shingled roof
And invited my attention.
I glanced where you pointed
With my mind full of tranquility.
Swiftly but with placid eyes,
Yes, you nodded at me.

Leaning against the soft knee
Of my sister beside me,
You were a tender infant.
Like your sister,
You smiled
At the tremor of the green shade of a fig tree
And brought happiness to the house
And to me,
Who had exhausted myself in poetry and literature.

The rough cruise has broken my oars
And I am adrift as an abandoned boat.
Deep in the bosom of someone who waits
There is a call from an everlasting fountain.
Waking here in early summer,
In a house however humble,
Expecting bliss to triumph over fate
And bring days of pride,
I sing to pass yesterday and today.
Hard though it may be to come up with the best poems,
The consolation is in the flood of bliss.

Suppose among a busy mob,

However lost I may be,
My world is a forest in a wide field of love
—Not a capital with rusty jails.
To see my sunflower,
The flowers of growing hope,
The orphans, wandering in a stoney field,
Vomiting blood at an elegy,
Will dream that the clouds play,
Will dream that the wind blesses the branches.
In this room with low windows
My soul is embraced softly
By the smell of burning incense.
Oh, at this sacred altar
I am proud to be a young monk.

My dear little sister,
Even if you live to see the day
When the majestic wood may wilt,
Admirable Holy Forest, Branches of Love:
In the tranquil song of mine
There is the tone of a peaceful dream.
When you become a mature woman,
Rubbing perfume in your hair,
The golden jewel in your shell-comb,
Then in your beauty and glory
When you tread on green grass
Forget not the felicity
Of the days with the gaunt man,
The poet with an ever-prosperous heart,
Together in an isolated hut.

A happiness beyond fate
To see days of sacred pride—
Burning incense in a broken censer
We delighted in singing songs.
Although the tone is of a low summer,
I have written with a happy heart
Of our happiness that summer.
My heart is committed to these eighty lines.
As my heart smiles,
Please receive them with a smile.

A White Face

The gray clouds flew in diffusion;
The west wind in late October roared through the branches;
Several hundred cherry-trees shed and scattered their leaves
　all at once.
From beyond the rain of the leaves,
To the other side—one glance, alas,
Casting only one glance toward me,
A girl passed swiftly.
Four years ago, late in autumn at the Ueno wood *
One desolate evening,
Beyond the rain of falling leaves,
Oh, one glance, a white face.

---

* A national park in Tokyo, known for its cherry blossoms.

Smoke (1)

As if I were ill,
I feel homesick today—
It is sad to find some smoke in the blue sky.

> There is no way of returning to the spring of a
>   fourteen-year-old
> When I used to call my name feebly
> And shed tears.

The smoke vanishing into the blue sky,
The smoke disappearing languidly,
Does it resemble me?

> The conductor of that train for that trip,
> Unexpectedly,
> Happened to be my junior-high classmate.

The refreshing water
Gushing out of a pump—
I watch it like a little boy.

Teachers and friends ignorantly
Blamed me
For my mysteriously neglected homework.

    I escaped through a classroom window
    And, alone,
    Went to lie in a ruin.

Lying on the lawn of a deserted castle
I was swallowed by the sky—
The feeling of a fifteen year-old boy.

    The flavor of things
    Which may be called sorrowful—
    I tasted it too early.

Whenever I looked up at a clear sky,
I longed to whistle;
And I amused myself by whistling.

    I whistled even in bed.
    The whistle
    Was my song when I was fifteen years old.

There was an instructor who scolded us often—
Because of his beard we called him a goat,
And we bleated at him.

> Yes, there was an army captain's son
> Who played with me,
> Throwing stones at small birds.

In the ruin of a castle
I sat on a stone
And relished a forbidden nut alone.

> Those friends who have abandoned me—
> In those days, we read together
> And we played together.

The autumn grass behind the school book-room—
A yellow flower grew there
Whose name I still don't know.

> When the flowers fell
> I was the first one
> To leave home in white clothes.

I used to be friends
With the brother of my late sister's boyfriend,
Which is sad to remember.

    There was a young instructor of English
    Who never came back
    From a summer vacation.

The memory of strikes
No longer excites my blood—
To my regret.

    At Morioka Junior High School,
    The banisters of its balcony—
    I wish I could lean against them again.

I dissuaded a fellow
From believing in God—
Yes, under a chestnut tree at that road-side.

    In a west wind
    Among the cherry leaves at Uchimaru Avenue
    We played, stepping on the fallen ones.

My favorite books of those days—
Most of them
Are no longer popular.

    Like a single stone
    Rolling down a hill
    I came down to this day.

With the envy of a discontent child
I watched birds fly
And watched them sing.

    Another grievous life:
    The dissected earthworm
    Under the wooden fence of the schoolyard.

My eyes ablaze with an infinite desire to learn—
My sister noted them with compassion
And asked me if I was in love with someone.

    The friends who advised me to read Sohō ◆
    Left school early
    Because of poverty.

◆ Sohō Tokutomi (1863–1957), a journalist, historian, and critic.

The learned instructor,
The droll movement of his hands—
Only I used to laugh.

> Another instructor told us
> About a man
> Whose talent ruined his life.

The idlest boy in the whole school
Is now
Working seriously.

> A friend of mine—
> Traveling, he cut an unsophisticated figure in the city,
> Only to return home in three days.

The girl who used to walk with me
Along a pine-tree avenue of Barajima
Was intelligent.

> I started wearing a pair of dark glasses for my eye
>   problem—
> Yes, it was then
> That I learned to cry alone.

My heart
Tends to cry secretly again—
All my friends have taken their own paths.

> As I found the tenderness and the sadness of love
> Earlier than anyone else,
> So I age before anyone else.

In excitement
My friend shed tears and waved his hand
And talked like a drunken villain.

> Struggling through a mob,
> My friend came up
> With the dear old thick cane.

He is the first person I wrote a New Year's card to—
Three years have passed
In this thought.

> Waking suddenly from a dream, I lament:
> Oh, my sleep,
> Why isn't it as pleasant as in my younger days?

The friend who was known for his intelligence
Is now in jail.
An autumn wind blows.

    Near-sighted,
    But he wrote droll songs—
    Shigeo's romance was also lamentable. *

My wife's old wishes
Were concerned with music—
Now she does not sing at all.

    One day all my friends scattered in four directions.
    Eight years later
    None has achieved fame.

This is the kind of day when I remember
The evening I first confessed my love
To my friend.

    My youth
    Flew off never to return,
    Like a kite with a broken string.

---

* In high school Takuboku formed a poetry club with Shigeo Kobayashi and others. Kobayashi, who later became a medical doctor, wrote many love letters to Takuboku's sister, Mitsuko.

A Feeble Thought

There is a torch feebly trembling.

Now, feebly my mind
Perceives the light in a cave
On a far island uninhabited.

There is a torch feebly trembling.

Now, feebly my mind
Perceives the feeling wet with tears
Of the person far away on a spring evening.

My thought trembles feebly.

Smoke (2)

I long to hear the dialect of my hometown—
Into the mob around a train station
I go to hear it.

> Like a sick beast,
> My heart
> Becomes meek upon hearing of my home.

Suddenly I realize—
For three years now I have not heard the sparrows
Which I used to hear daily in my hometown.

> I pick up the geography book
> Which my late professor
> Gave me a long time ago.

The ball I threw on a school roof
A long time ago,
I wonder how it is now.

The abandoned stone on the road-side
In my hometown—
Was it buried under the grass again this year?

> As we live far away from each other, I miss my sister—
> She was a child who would cry
> Asking for a pair of geta-shoes with red straps. ◆

Two days ago I saw a picture of a mountain.
And this morning
I suddenly long for the mountains of home.

> A candy vendor's whistle,
> I pick it out
> Along with my boyhood innocence.

Now and then
My mother talks about our village—
Yes, it is autumn already.

> Unintentionally,
> We start talking about our village—
> Ah, the smell of rice cake being toasted on an autumn
>   evening.

◆ Clogs typically made of paulownia wood.

For some reason I long for Shibutami Village—
The dear mountains,
The dear rivers.

>   Today is one of those days when I feel sympathy
>   For the people in my hometown—
>   They sell their fields to drink to their own ruin.

Alas, those children I have taught—
They will also
Quit their homeland.

>   Nothing is more sad
>   Than to see the children from a country town
>   Rejoicing over their reunion in a city.

The regret of having left my hometown
As though driven away with stones—
It stays with me, never to be lost.

>   The soft green willows
>   On the Kitakami River bank—
>   They seem to ask me to cry with them.

A village doctor's wife in my hometown,
The modest pile of her hair in a comb
Illuminates my memory.

> The cheap hotel
> Managed by the fellow
> Who used to compete with me for our school's
>   highest honor.

Chiyoji, as well as others, grew up to experience romance   ♦
And achieved some children,
Just as I did during my journey.

> I remember the woman
> Who offered to rent me some clothes
> So that I could join the Bon Festival dance.   ♦♦

With a retarded brother
And a deformed father, Santa is pitiable—   ♦♦♦
He reads till late at night.

> Oh, the stealing habit of the motherless child—
> He used to canter
> A bay pony with me.

♦ According to Takuboku's diary, a mad man who jumped up and down to see an evening star.
♦♦ A summer festival for the dead, featuring lively folk dancing.
♦♦♦ Not Santa Claus but a common name for the third son of a family.

The large design of red flowers—
I remember her clothes
And my romance at six years of age.

    After his name has been forgotten,
    The man casually returned home
    And coughed.

The carpenter's vicious boy, too, is pitiable—
He went to war
Never to return alive.

    The sordid land-owner's first son
    With consumption—
    The spring thunder on his wedding day.

Okane was crying
As she begged Sōjirō for some money—
At dusk with white radish flowers.

    The cowardly village clerk—
    There was a rumor about his insanity
    One autumn in my hometown.

My cousin: being bored with hunting,
He drank, sold his house,
And died from illness.

>The fellow who went on a drunken rampage—
>When I went to take his hands
>He was pacified and wept endlessly.

When drunk,
This instructor drew a sword to chase after his wife;
He was banished from the town.

>Year after year, tuberculosis increased;
>They invited a young doctor
>To the village.

For lightning-bug hunting
I said I would go to a river;
This man took me to a mountain road.

>The rain in a city
>Reminded me of the rain
>On the light-purple potato flowers.

The policemen's urchins
Are also pitiable—
They have no friends to play with.

    Today I hear
    That the unfortunate bachelor
    Is indulging in a sordid love affair.

For my sake,
To tranquilize my suffering soul,
A woman sang a hymn.

    The young woman
    Who first preached Jesus Christ's teachings
    In our village. ✦

The train window—
When the mountains of my country appear in the far north,
I straighten my collar.

    As I step on the soil of my country
    My feet become somewhat lighter
    And my heart grows heavier.

✦ The reference is to Chieko Tachibana, one of eight female instructors at Shibutani Village Elementary School, where Takuboku worked as a substitute teacher.

The moment I enter my hometown,
I feel hurt at the sight of wider roads
And new bridges.

> A woman instructor, a stranger,
> Stands at the window
> Of my alma mater.

In that very house, at that very window,
On a spring evening,
I heard the croaking of frogs with my Hideko. *

> The nickname, "Genius," from my younger days
> Distresses me now—
> That is why I cry in my hometown.

I picked up a pebble under a walnut-tree
At the bank of a river
By a train station of my town.

> Facing the mountains in my hometown,
> I am silent—
> How grateful I am to those mountains!

---

* Hideko Hotta, Takuboku's second-grade teacher.

You, Flower

You, Red Rosebud—
Through a pale silk cover
Your color softly radiates.
Wondering what to do,
I raise the sleeve of my black robe;
Through the veil of my sleeve, even more powerfully,
Your perfume penetrates.

Unable to contain the color,
The blood of life burns my cheeks.
Unable to seal the scent,
Starry perfume floats in my eyes.
My artless desire
Like the burning wick of an oil lamp
Illuminates you, flower.

In Response to a Pleasant Autumn Wind

A puddle
Reflects the evening sky and a red ribbon,
After an autumn rain.

> A crossroad in autumn—
> The wind that blows down three of the four roads
> Leaves no trace.

The familiar mountains—
As each autumn comes,
I examine them to see if a god lives there.

> Gently, the rain falls—
> As I watch the garden gradually getting wet,
> My tears dry.

The millet leaves rustle loudly—
I miss the eaves of my home in the country
When the autumn wind blows.

When I am starving
A begging dog's face looks dear—
It gazes at me, wagging its thin tail.

    Since heaven knows when,
    I have forgotten how to cry—
    Would someone please come make me cry?

The melancholy brought on by sakē
Suffused my mind—
I will stand up and dance awhile.

    A cricket sings—
    Sitting on a stone beside it
    I talk to myself with a tearful smile.

Since the time when I grew weak in sickness
I have formed the habit
Of sleeping with my mouth half open.

    The mistake of immaturity—
    I considered triumph over one person
    To be my grand goal.

The resentful expression
Of her soft glance—
I love it, but oh, how coldly she treats me!

    With the pleasure of meeting
    A long-forgotten friend,
    I listen to the sound of water.

Like my father, the autumn is severe;
Like my mother, the autumn is tender;
For a homeless child.

    Like a bow readily curved in an autumn rain,
    Lately
    You have been hard to get along with.

The autumn evening has come—
My sorrow and moonlight
Fill heaven and earth.

    As a vagabond sleeps in his hometown,
    So quietly
    Winter has come.

The Illusion of Cherry Blossoms

"Under heaven, nobody is a stranger.
 My yearning for you, poet,
 Brought me down spring roads of one-thousand *ri*."
 A girl's voice with a sweet southern accent spoke.
 I looked up and saw a branch of cherry blossoms in full bloom
 In a small pail by the window
 Of my deserted hut.

"I'm just a country girl from the north,
 But I will clean your yard in the morning
 So you can make spring poems."
 A nightingale's voice spoke at the edge of a bamboo grove.
 Looking up, I saw a cherry stump
 Laden with cottony pink flowers.

"My sick brother sent me as a spring messenger
 From the Tsukushi fields far west
 To have you comment on his poetry collection."
 A voice rang
 As if fragrant flower dewdrops
 Dripped onto the grass.
 Looking up, I saw by my well
 A young cherry tree handsomely in bloom
 With the color of innocent compassion.

"Have you forgotten, Sir, have you,
 The child you left in the northern country of Shinogi?
 Though your letter did not say, 'come,'

* One *ri* is approximately 2,400 miles.

Yet at the invitation of the spring wind,
Led by the blooming flowers and the full spring,
Thinking that there is no reason
To live alone acting sour,
Following the eastern road
I have come for a visit."
Another voice gently stroked my cheeks like a sweet breeze.
Then my delighted gaze caught sight of
A large tree full of the blossoms of wisdom
Standing by my eastern window.
The smiling sun brimmed over
The flowers onto my manuscript
Laid out on my desk
To color it gold.

"There are days of great happiness
Even to this impoverished poet," so saying
I put down my pen with a smile.
Presently, a breeze blew off the clouds of flowers
As if playing with my illusory cherry nymphs.
In the window and on the yard
It sprinkled pink flowers for some time.

A Crossroad

The old and the young,
Scores of them, male and female,
From east and from west,
Down the hill, up the hill,
Each for each, in a rush
Pass this point.
The point where I now stand
Is the junction
Of four streets overlooking a sea.
—All the houses at the crossing
Have stern appearances:
A banker's residence, a consul's residence,
A newspaper company. And the other building is
A police station where they keep a black dog
To pursue people, sniffing their crimes.

Whoever crosses this point—everybody, look at him!—
Goes with others, forming a group.
Disregarding the sun in the high sky,
Disregarding the boat-filled sea.
But watching somebody else's house,
And silently, he walks on somebody else's road.
A white-haired old man, as well.
A young maiden with a silk parasol.
Boys, too, with loud footsteps.
A fisherman smoking a cigarette,
A tall gentleman, and
A skinny woman with a grandchild on her back.

A merchant, fat from alcohol, throwing his stomach forward,
A beggar-urchin,
A young waiter whistling,
And the unfortunate people without a house.

They pass here in a rush.
At the wide crossing, despite the multitude of people,
Nobody seems to know each other.
Though walking side by side, though they meet again,
They all pretend not to know one another.
Each for each and in his own way
They rush, competing with one another.

The soulless trees in a forest
Cross their branches as they lean against one another;
Even the leaves which fall and die at the end of a year
Whisper in a morning breeze
And talk in the evening wind.
The human world is a scattered forest.
The human world is an uninhabited desert.
Indeed, myself, I go on my way;
I had no comrade all day long.
At the crossing, as I paced
And measured my steps,
With a loud bang of the door
From the newspaper company on the right,
Ringing the bells tied to their belts,
Some men rushed out onto the four roads.
Now in the month of May, on a clear day,
No cloud shutters the sun,

No wave roars in the sea,
But in the busy human world
Something must have happened.

The Moon and the Gong

> *A song made for my friend to be sung
> to the accompaniment of koto music.*

To prolong the remaining music
Of my distant homeland,
The moonlight on a cherry field
Spreads the faint color of dream.
Amidst the slumber of the cherry blossoms
A child's wonder forms no dream.
To lead him into a sweet dream
Does the evening gong sing to the moon?

◆ A koto is six-foot-long harp with thirteen strings, laid on the floor when played.

To a Takuboku Bird

> *It came from somewhere I do not know.*
> *On October the ninth, it sat on an old*
> *plumtree trunk less than ten steps away*
> *from me. It pecked away at the tree*
> *without being troubled by my presence.*

Bird, why did you come here?
No matter how hard your beak may be,
No matter how hard you peck though the day
At the sinful caterpillars
Nestling like guilty criminals
Inside the murky old tree-trunks,
You won't be able to eat them all.
Your food must be
In the very marrow of the tree of life.
The trees that were untouched by axes,
The trees that chronicled the ancients' lives
As they were vivified by white clouds and evening glows,
Have pierced heaven for eight-thousand years.
Bird, why did you come here?
This is the place
For an abandoned child to find consolation
Leaning against the cold pillar,
His eyes watery
From the heat of the dim, descending sun—
A sinful home
Where one sucks the mild perfume

---

* *Takuboku* is Japanese for woodpecker. Takuboku adopted this pen-name for himself in 1903.

Of the spiritual flower only in his dreams.
—I envy you.
O bird, why did you come here?

August

The sand-hill extends long, and
The August sun reflects off it; the sand steams.
The strong smell of seaweed floats.
In ecstasy, drunk in the sun,
The beach-sparrows sing
In high tones.

No cloud flies in the open sky. On the open pasture
The wide green patch of summer grass
Crawls in the sun; far in the roaring sea
The lazy sailboats gambol
Like a group of sheep.

When I walk, the sand feels pleasant.
As an isolated vagabond,
At the hubbub of the breaking and retreating wave,
I thought of my mother's beach
Far away in my home country.

The secluded beach of a shiny sandy island—
I, to collect some seashells, and my mother, to collect
Some seaweed, we went there together.
So beautiful were Augusts in my childhood,
Blessed by the morning breeze
From the green field with balmy beach-lotus.

A Willow Leaf

A willow leaf which perched on my lap,
Coming through a train window—

Here, too, is degeneration.
Yes, this woman, too,
Has been following a destined road—

The woman dozing off in the next seat
With a travel-bag on her lap,
Exhausted, sorrowful but attractive—
Where are you going?

After an Endless Discussion

We read more and we discuss more
And thus our eyes glitter brighter
Than did the Russian youth of fifty years ago.
We discuss what we must do.
However, no one pounds on the table
And declares, "V NARÓD!" ◆

We know what we seek,
We know what people seek,
And we know what we must do.
We, in fact, know more than did the Russian youth of fifty
  years ago.
We discuss what we must do.
However, no one pounds on the table
And declares, "V NARÓD!"

This is an assembly of youth,
The youth who create new things.
We know that we triumph when our elders die.
Observe the brightness of our eyes , the heat of our discussion.
However, no one pounds on the table
And declares, "V NARÓD!"

At last, the candles are renewed for the third time,
And dead insects float in our teacups;
Though the enthusiasm is no less than that of young women,
There is a fatigue in the youths' eyes after a long discussion,
And still, no one pounds on the table
And declares, "V NARÓD!"

◆ Russian for "Go to the People!"

An Epitaph

We have always respected him
And we continue to respect him,
Though two months have passed since we interred him
Under a chestnut-tree in that suburban cemetery.
Yes, two months have already passed
Since we ceased to see him at our meetings.
He did not argue,
But he was an indispensable person.

One day he said,
"Comrades, do not blame me for my silence.
I am unable to argue,
But I am always ready to rise."
As a member described him:
"His eyes readily accuse the theorist's cowardice."
I have often judged him likewise,
But now we no longer receive accusations against injustice
  from his eyes.

He was a laborer—a technician.
He always worked enthusiastically and cheerfully.
During his free hours, he talked with his fellows and read much.
He neither smoked nor drank.

His serious, valiant, and prudent character
Reminded us of Bakunin's friend in those Jura mountains.
Attacked by a violent fever, and lying in bed,
He did not mumble even in deathbed.

"Today is May Day, Our Day,"
  These were the last words he left with me.
  In the morning of that day I visited him at the hospital.
  In the evening of that day, he finally entered his eternal sleep.

  Ah, his high forehead, hammer-like brawny arms,
  And his courage to face death as readily as he faced life—
  His straight stare into our soul as well—
  Emerge before me when I close my eyes.

  His corpse, as a materialist's, was buried under that chestnut-tree.
  The epitaph which we, his fellows, selected for him is as follows:
"I am always ready to rise."

A Fist

Being pitied by a wealthier person
Or being laughed at by a stronger person,
Impulsively, I raised my fist.
But a peaceful spirit,
Meek like a criminal's,
Squatted in a nook of my humiliated mind
With an innocent blinking of her eyes:
Distrust in myself.
Oh, distrust in myself!
With the fist already up,
You,
Whom will you strike?
Your friend or yourself
Or the innocent wall beside you?

Don't Wake Up

There is a life more insipid
Than the dusty window glass
Heated by the western sun.

Exhausted by long thinking,
Dripping perspiration,
He snores during his nap.
In the young man's mouth yellow teeth appear;
The summer light through the glass window shines on his
    hairy leg
And a flea creeps on it.

Don't wake up, don't wake up, until the day is done—
Until a cool and calm evening visits your life.
A woman's erotic laughter somewhere.

Unforgettable People (1)

Those shore-roses on the sandy hills
Of the northern shore with fresh wind—
I wonder if they are blooming this year.

    Counting the few years I have lived
    And looking at my fingers,
    I come to dread traveling.

The names of the towns I saw through the train window
A few times
Seem dear to me.

    I remembered
    A barber's apprentice at Hakodate—
    It was pleasant to have him shave around my ears.

My mother and my wife followed me and came to live
In an isolated land
Where we had no acquaintances.

◆ Takuboku worked in the city of Hakodate in 1907 as a substitute teacher and freelance reporter.

Thinking of the sea in Tsugaru,
I recall my sister's eyes
Dull from seasickness.

    The story of his younger days,
    That he rubbed some dung on a bridge rail—
    He related it to me in reminiscence.

The friend who laughed at me
That I would not marry for the rest of my life
Is not married yet.

    That precious woman instructor—
    The brim of her glasses
    Used to shine desolately.

A friend gave me some rice—
How hopeless I was
To have refused it!

    Aoyigi City in Hakodate is dear to me—
    My friend's love song,
    The bluebottle flowers.

Smelling
The paper of a new foreign book,
I longed suddenly for some money.

    The series of thoughts
    At Ōmori Beach in Hakodate
    Where the white waves rushed and roared...

I remember my favorite alarm clock
Which played a Chinese popular song
Morning after morning.

    The writing in the manuscript,
    The unsuccessful essay on the grief of my wandering
       life—
    Oh, I can hardly read it again.

The Chinese poem on the monument
Halfway up Gagyū Mountain, Hakodate—
I have forgotten half of it.

    Ambiguously,
    A beggar mumbled
    Something possibly important.

As if asking others to think little of him,
A divine friend
Entered a mountain.

> The place
> Where dropouts gather and drink
> Turned out to be my own home.

A friend of mine
Who became a young father of several children
Sings as if childless when he is drunk.

> Holding my yawning,
> I bade farewell at a train window—
> The departure seems now somewhat insipid.

The old scar on the cheek of a woman
Who got off the train at Kuchian Station
At midnight . . .

> The sorrow I brought to Sapporo
> That autumn—
> I still have it.

An autumn evening
On a quiet wide street,
The fragrance of some grilled corn ...

    The rain in Sapporo—
    I spent the first night
    Listening to a quarrel between two sisters.

The well-known beautiful station of Ishikari—
A red cloth was hung on the fence
To be dried.

    Otaru is a sad town—
    The coarse voices
    Of the never-singing people.

Shaking his head as if crying,
A fortune-teller asked me
To show my palm.

    A friend of mine
    Who came to borrow a little money—
    Snowflakes on his back ...

I remember being told
That all my skinny body
Was a lump of rebellious spirit.

> The person who wrote the article on the first snow
> Of that year and for that paper
> Was myself.

The drunkenness of that fellow
Who lifted a chair and prepared to strike me—
I suppose he is sober by now.

> I lost in the fight—
> Now I suspect
> The cause was myself.

When he said he would not strike me,
I insisted that he should—
Yes, I used to be a different man.

> The fellow I quarreled with
> And parted from with bitter hatred—
> I miss him today.

There was a friend who had my wife sew his clothes,
Since winter comes early
In the colony.

    With his palm
    The fellow wiped his face, made wet by a snowstorm.
    He was a communist.

Another friend of mine
Went to Sakhalin
To start a new religion.

    The days were good
    When we said
    That we were bored with the peaceful and uneventful world.

The friend who wished
To open a cooperative drugstore—
I hear he is a swindler now.

    Tears shining on his pale cheeks,
    He talked of death—
    Oh, that young merchant!

With our baby on her back,
She saw me off at a snow-blown station—
Oh, my wife's eyebrows!

> With the fellow I hated as an enemy
> I shook hands for a long time,
> Since it was his departure.

From the window of a slowly departing train
I drew my head back before anybody else did,
Because of my pride.

> The voyage is lamentable
> When I think of the reputation I leave behind.
> It is like a voyage into a grave.

After parting, when I blinked,
Unexpectedly
Something cold ran on my cheeks.

> Though the place is unfamiliar except for the name,
> The cheap lodging fee
> Makes me feel at home.

The politician who traveled with me—
It was sad to see him sleep,
Looking pale with his mouth open.

> The lodging place
> Where I stayed to cry heartily—
> The lukewarmness of their tea.

Sorachi River, buried in the snow—
No bird was visible,
But there was a man in the forest by the bank.

> Hopelessly exhausted by the train ride,
> What I think intermittently about
> Is the preciousness of myself.

I still remember
The young stationmaster's mild eyes—
He called the station's name in a musical tone.

> Getting off at a station in a wasteland,
> The light shone on the snow—
> I have come to a lonely town.

Gracefully the ice glistens,
And the plovers sing
Under the winter moon at the Kushiro Sea.

> While I warm a frozen ink bottle
> Over the fire,
> My tears run under lamplight.

His face and his voice,
Only those reminded me of the friend I used to know
When I met him at the end of the country.

> A sudden burst of a woman's laughter
> Penetrated to my ear
> At midnight when wine might freeze in the kitchen.

I wonder what has happened to the woman
Who stopped singing,
Being offended by my drunkenness.

> Among other things, I also do not forget the creamy
>   earlobe
> Of a woman
> Called Koyakko.

* A name meaning "Little Servant," often used for geishas.

Leaning against each other,
Standing in the midnight snow,
Oh, the warmth of the woman's hand.

>   When I asked if she wanted to die,
>   The woman showed me
>   A scar on her throat.

Being asked, I stood up and danced,
Helplessly,
Until I fell in heavy drunkenness.

>   Waiting till I was dead drunk,
>   A person whispered to me
>   About various sorrows.

The sorrow is
The mark of my kiss
On that white soft arm.

>   When I turned my head in drunkenness,
>   And when I opened my eyes to have some water,
>   I called her name.

Like an insect seeking fire,
I formed a habit
Of visiting lighted houses.

> Squeak, squeak, the floor squeaks in the cold;
> A sudden kiss in the hallway
> On my way home.

Resting my head on her lap—
Oh, my mind,
It is concerned only with myself.

> They say he died lately,
> My competitor in love—
> He was a man of tremendous intelligence.

A friend made senile by his wandering—
He recited a Chinese poem which he had written ten years
  before
When he was drunk.

> The cold air
> Which closes my nostrils with ice—
> I feel like inhaling it again.

In the February harbor with no waves,
A white foreign boat
Floats low.

>On a night with a heavy snow,
>A girl screamed as though her house were on fire
>When a string of her shamisen broke. *

The evening when I sang to the shamisen of a woman
Who had tried to commit suicide
In her hometown.

>An old purple notebook—
>The date and the place
>Of our secret tryst.

There are some memories
As unpleasant
As a pair of dirty socks.

>The day when I remember the event,
>The woman crying in my room,
>As if it had been in a fiction.

---

* A musical instrument with three strings on a long fingerboard, played with a large plectrum.

An Old Man

In a bleak cold corner of the house
There is a small room never opened.
A bony old man with hollow eyes
Sits there alone.

In the darkness, alas, days and nights,
Motionless, he remains half-asleep.
Slothful are the turbid coughs
In the mornings and at night.

Now and then he mutters something.
He curls his lips to form a cold smile.
And, crunch, crunch,
He chews a piece of bone.

Shamelessly, crunch, crunch—
Alas, it is the white bone
Of his first love who, for many years,
Lies dead in his heart!

Now and then, he folds his trembling fingers
To count something.
Sometimes, he counts the number of friends
Who have betrayed him, and at other times

The memory of his old friends
From whom he parted, holding their warm hands.
The memory of the long road in his hometown, as well,
From which he has run away alone.

One day, he seems to tell himself,
"There is something. Look at the sky."
But he answers later, "There is nothing."
"Indeed, it is true, all is vain," he laughs.

Unforgettable People (2)

As a traveler from afar
With frozen cheeks,
I asked only the direction to a certain place.

> My nonchalant remark—
> You seem to have taken it nonchalantly;
> That was all.

The dark eyes
Absorbing only the pleasant part of the world
Are still fresh in my memory.

> Though I have the word now
> Which I failed to say then
> . . . .

Like a scratch on a white lampshade,
It is impossible to erase
The memory of exile.

> The regret of the night
> I left the burnt place in Hakodate
> Lingers in my mind.

Even when I forget,
Something accidental brings it back.
No, it is impossible to forget.

> Sympathize
> With my throbbing heart
> When I see somebody who reminds me of you
>   in town.

I thought this morning again
That if only I could hear your voice again
My mind would be pacified.

> The occasional thought of this kind
> That crops up in the middle of my busy life—
> To whom is it due?

If a friend opened his mind
Meditatively,
He would certainly talk about you.

    Suddenly
    Thinking about you,
    Alas, my tranquil mind is disturbed.

Many years have passed since we parted.
Each year makes you
Dearer to me.

    Your house
    On the outskirts of Ishikari City—
    The apple blossoms must be falling now.

The long letters—
Three of them came in three years.
I think I have written four.

When I Take My Gloves Off

Suddenly, I rest my hands while taking off my gloves.
Some memory
Passed through my mind.

> Sometime in the past
> I learned to dissemble my feelings.
> It must have been about when I began to grow my
>   beard.

During the morning bath,
Resting my neck on the rim of the bathtub,
I breathe slowly and release my nerves.

> On summer mornings
> Gargle stings my bad tooth—
> The fresh pain is enjoyable.

Staring closely at my hands,
I remember
The woman who was good at kissing.

Blaming my eyes
For being unaccustomed to many colors,
I sent somebody to buy some red flowers.

    The pleasure of
    Buying a new book and reading it in the evening—
    I have long since forgotten.

When I come home
After a seven-day trip,
The red ink on my window appears so dear.

    The dirty blotter
    Which I found in an old book
    Makes me feel good.

The touch of the snow melting in my hand
Feels good.
It penetrates to my mind, tired of sleeping.

    The fading shadow on the shōji-screen—
    As I see it,
    My heart gradually grows dark.

The cool smell of medicine
Prevails at night
In the house where a doctor used to live.

    The old hat
    I have worn daily for six years
    Is now hard to abandon.

To eyes
Which have indulged in a pleasant spring slumber
The grass in the garden appears tender.

    A spring snow
    Falls gently
    On the three-story brick building in a Ginza alley. *

On a filthy brick wall
The spring snow
Falls and melts and falls and melts.

    On the window
    Which a girl with bad eyes leans against,
    Softly, a spring rain falls.

---

* A famous shopping street in Tokyo.

The smell of fresh trees
Fills the air—
The stillness of spring in a new town.

      A spring town,
      The tempting door plates on women's houses—
      I walk around and read their names.

From somewhere
The smell of burned tangerine rind
Brought back to me an evening.

      The voices
      From a busy young women's group
      Make me feel lonely.

White plates,
A neglected woman in a corner of a bar—
She wipes each dish and piles it on a shelf.

      Somewhere
      In an avenue of a dry winter,
      The smell of carbolic acid is mingled.

The smell of vinegar
On a fresh salad plate
Penetrates to my mind on a quiet evening.

    The trembling hand is endearing
    As it pours some goat milk
    Out of a sky-colored bottle.

The smell of a piece of ham
Left in the evening
In a kitchen suddenly hushed.

    In front of a rack loaded with regularly-placed bottles,
    A woman picks her teeth—
    A sorry sight.

Exchanging a rather long kiss, I came home
Late at night
And I saw a fire in the distance.

    The white face
    At an evening window of a hospital
    Was slightly familiar to me.

When was it?
I remember the dancer
On board a pleasure boat at Ōkawa.

> While writing a long unnecessary letter
> I suddenly miss somebody
> And go downtown.

As I smoke a wet cigarette
Most of my thoughts
Also become slightly wet.

> Acutely,
> Feeling the approach of summer,
> I smell the rain-wet earth in a small garden.

In the show-window of a glass shop
Decorated to look cool and refreshing
I see the moon on a summer night.

> Hearing of your coming,
> I get up early and
> Worry about the stain on my white shirt.

The nervous manner of my young friend—
Lately
His dull eyes make me feel sorry.

       Somewhere there is a sound of a stake being driven in.
       There is a sound of a large barrel being rolled.
       And it started snowing.

In a deserted office at night,
Wildly,
A telephone rang, and it stopped.

       Talking voices past midnight—
       I open my eyes
       And I begin hearing them after awhile.

The clock stopped as I watched it—
As if being absorbed by the void,
My heart, again, runs to solitude.

       The gargle I use
       Every morning—
       The bottle is cold since autumn has come.

On a path at the foot of a hill
With a smooth slope of green barley
I found a small comb.

    In the cedar bush on a mountainside
    A sparse shadow creeps
    On an autumn afternoon.

A harbor town—
The sea-cloud presses down
The kite circling with a dull cry.

    A newspaper office
    At Takiyama-chō in Kyōbashi district—
    The bustle in the evening light.

My father who used to scold me all the time—
He no longer scolds me.
I wish he would scold me.

    A willow leaf
    Which a morning wind blew to my train—
    I pick it up and look at it.

For no reason, I longed for a sea.
I came to a sea
On the day when my heart ached so.

    A red sash excited my wearied eyes
    When I turned them away
    From a smooth sea.

Today was such a day
That all the women I met in town
Returned home with a broken heart.

    A train trip,
    A small station in the middle of a field—
    The smell of the summer grass recalls my earlier days.

The train which I barely caught for an early autumn trip
Early in the morning—
How hard the bread was that I had to eat!

    By a window during that train trip
    I thought
    How lamentable my future would be.

Looking up,
I noticed that the clock had stopped at a station in a forest—
A train ride on a rainy evening.

    Having parted from her,
    Inside a dim train window,
    I play idly with my green apple.

The desperate atmosphere of the bar
Which I visit habitually—
The twilight shines red through my wine.

    Like a lotus in a marsh,
    My sorrow
    Floats clearly in my drunken awareness.

Through the wall
I hear a young woman cry—
Oh, the autumn mosquito-net of an inn.

    The familiar smell of last year's winter clothes—
    It makes me meditative
    On an early autumn morning.

The pain in my left knee which I worried about
Has been forgotten since I don't know when.
An autumn wind blows.

> Selling my books one by one,
> I have only a soiled German dictionary left
> At the end of the summer.

With the fellow I used to hate passionately for no reason
I have somehow become intimate—
The autumn advances.

> The day has come to search
> Through the bottom of my wicker trunk
> For the nationally-banned, worn, red-covered book.

In the street, I met the author
Of a book currently banned:
Yes, on an autumn morning.

> Since the day
> When I decided to drink
> The autumn wind began to blow.

The wife of a friend of mine—
Only her watery eyes and the mole below her eyes
Attract my attention.

> She was a girl
> Who, whenever I saw her, rolled a ball of yarn
> To knit a sock.

In a field in daylight
Where some insects squeak faintly here and there,
I read a letter.

> Late at night I opened a door
> To find something white running in my garden.
> It may have been a dog.

A faint pink reflected on the window panes
At two o' clock in the morning.
Oh, the soundless color of a fire.

> The evening—
> When the smell of an onion mingles with
> The sorrow which soaks my body...

The house of the thirty-year-old bachelor—
Now and then
He imitates a cat and laughs about it.

> Like a cowardly scout,
> Nervously,
> I took a walk alone late at night.

The quiet town asleep;
All my skin turns to ears;
My heavy footsteps.

> A man without a hat—
> He entered a station late at night
> And stood and sat around, only to leave soon.

When I realize
The town is wet with evening dew,
I have, indeed, wandered long.

> With a derelict
> Who asked me if I had a cigarette to spare
> I talked late at night.

As if coming back from a wild field,
I came home
After a solitary walk in the night in Tokyo.

    The blue ink
    Spilt on the frosted flagstone
    Below a bank's window...

In the morning air of October,
For the first time,
A baby breathed.

    The pacing to and fro
    In the long wet hallway
    Of a gynecologist's office in October...

There was a thought
Tender like the touch of an infant
When I walked in a park alone.

    That face is unforgettable—
    The smiling face of the man
    Who was arrested by an officer in town today.

I lit a match,
And through the two-foot circle of light
A white moth flew.

    My friend wanders today again
    Carrying a motherless baby on his back
    In that ruin of a castle.

Late at night,
Coming home from work,
I hold my baby who has just died.

    They say the baby let out a cry or two
    Just before dying—
    My tears run.

When the white root of daikon-radish ripened,
A baby was born
Only to die soon.

    Of all the late autumn air
    My baby breathed only four square-feet
    Before he died.

All our attention was focused on the doctor's hand
When he inserted the syringe
Into the dead infant's chest.

> As if facing an unfathomable mystery,
> I place my hand
> On the baby's forehead.

The sorrow
Of not having a strong pang
When my child's body grows colder.

> Alas,
> The warmth in my dead child
> Remained until the dawn came.

No Title (1)

Roof after roof, as far as my vision reaches,
The roofs leave no gap in-between!
Round roofs, tall roofs, and squashed roofs—
Some cling to the ground to escape from the crush,
Others try to escape into the sky!
Above them all, like a dutiful instructor's eyes,
The autumn light shines warmly.

Uncapturable,
And yet shaking the foundation of our soul,
Oh, the roaring of the city—
When I first saw this scene
And when I first heard this noise,
My weak rustic's heart was intimidated
Neither by the width nor by the height
Nor by the nobility of the civilization lurking there,
But by the depth of the night in the city—
In the ever-lower bottom of that infinite noise.

Now I come here again, to see the scene again,
To hear the noise again,
And my weak immigrant's heart is intimidated—
The feeling of a lion-keeper seeing his lion asleep—
I am in the ever-lower bottom of an elusive noise—
The farther I enter, the farther yet I have to go
Into the depth of the night in the city.

My dutiful instructor,
You who regards all your students' desires as one,

Do you also consider your students' and your desire to be one?

Flowers fall exuding their scented seminal fluid,
Men die perspiring their vital force—
Do they live only for that?

Sad Toys

When I breathe,
I hear a sound rattling in my chest—
A sound more merciless than a biting winter wind.

> Closing my eyes,
> I see nothing in my heart.
> Desolate, I open my eyes again.

Being thirsty,
I went out to look for a fruit shop still open
Late at night in autumn.

> My child has not yet returned from playing outside.
> I pull out and try to run
> Her toy engine.

"I want to buy a book, I want to buy a book."
Though I don't intend to blame her,
I say this to my wife again.

The husband's thought—all about traveling;
The scolding and crying of the wife!
A breakfast table!

    Though I have walked
    About six-hundred yards from my house
    As if I had a destination to reach ...

Dear old winter morning—
When I drink some boiled water
The steam gently covers my face.

    For no particular reason
    I feel a little cheerful this morning—
    I cut my fingernails.

The agreeableness of a refreshing recovery from drunkenness!
I get up at night
And get ready for calligraphy.

    I fear my recent reckless attitude
    Of surrendering all my hopes
    To the course of my fate.

I feel as though all my limbs were detached.
An unpleasant awakening!
A sad awakening!

    Spreading a cheap newspaper from my hometown,
    I found some misprints—
    The sorrow of this morning.

I wish somebody
Would scold me to his heart's content.
What does this mean?

    Every morning
    I rub and grieve
    The light numbness of the thigh I slept on.

Like a train dashing through an open field
This anguish
Passes through my mind.

    Without any particular reason,
    As though to prostrate myself before my first love's
       grave,
    I came to the suburbs.

There arose the illusion of returning
To my dear hometown
When I took a train after a long while.

    Although there's no lie
    In the words
    That I believe in a new tomorrow …

When I think deeply,
There is and there is not a thing I really desire;
I polish my pipe.

    I look at my dirty hands—
    It is exactly
    The way I face my heart lately.

The slight satisfaction
Of washing my dirty hands
Is the satisfaction for today.

    Driven by a sudden yearning,
    I came to a mountain.
    I look for the stone I sat on last year.

I overslept and did not read the morning paper.
It weighs on me, as usual,
Like a debt.

> The relaxed feeling of a new year!
> Vacantly,
> I feel I have forgotten all my past.

In vain I try to remember
My attitude up to yesterday
When I strived from morning till night.

> As if forecasting the happiness of this year,
> Somehow
> The sky on New Year's Day is bright and calm.

From the bottom of my stomach
I yawned for a long time
On New Year's Day this year.

> A friend of mine—
> He writes on his New Year's card
> A few similar poems every year.

On January the fourth,
From that person,
I received the annual postcard.

> My head,
> Which thinks only of the impossible things in the
>   world—
> Shall I continue to scold it this year?

Everybody else
Is heading in the same direction,
But my mind stares at them from aside.

> Until when
> Must I keep this picture-frame hung on the wall?
> I am tired of seeing it.

Gradually,
As a candle melts down,
The night has come on the last day of the year.

> Leaning against a blue Seto brazier ◆
> I open and close my eyes,
> Regretting the passage of time.

◆ A glazed ceramic pot used for heating.

I feel that happiness is coming tomorrow—
I go to sleep
Scolding my throbbing heart.

    Did the fatigue of the past year come
    On New Year's Day?
    I doze off.

Tucking myself in a futon mattress
And folding my legs,
I stick out my tongue at nobody in particular.

    Somehow, New Year's Day has gone by
    And my life
    Has returned to the same old rut.

I argued with God and wept—
Oh, that dream!
It was a morning about four days ago.

    I worked all day again today,
    Considering the time to go home
    As the only thing to look forward to.

I could not fathom
The thoughts of various people.
I spent another quiet day.

    The various things
    I thought I would do—
    If I were the editor of this newspaper!

Ah! The butter
Sent by a farmer's bride
Of Sorachi County in Ishikari Prefecture.

    Many of the peasants, I hear, have given up drinking.
    If they became harder up,
    What would they give up?

How sensitive my heart is upon waking!
Tears fall
Even at the news of an old man running away from home.

    Waking
    With the thought
    That I can never cooperate with other people!

The person who shares a thought with me
And yet
Who appears to be unexpectedly heavy-handed.

    For half a day
    I lectured my junior,
    And I am all weary.

Unusually for me today,
Tears welled up while I was cursing the Congress.
I am happy to find some emotion left in me.

    Wishing to make flowers blossom overnight,
    I warmed the cherry plant over the fire,
    All in vain.

By mistake, I broke a rice bowl.
I think again this morning
Of the pleasure of breaking things.

    Suddenly, I felt miserable;
    Repeatedly scolding my cowardice,
    I go to borrow some money.

An old newspaper—
Look, there is an article praising my poems,
Though it's only a few lines.

    I did not realize then
    But there are many misspellings
    In my old love letters.

The bunch of my wife's letters
Of eight years ago—
I am worried as to its whereabouts.

    The sadness of my chronic insomnia!
    Even when I feel only slightly sleepy,
    I sleep in agitation.

I could not quite laugh, though I wanted to,
When I found the lost knife
In my own hand.

    These several years
    I have not looked up at the sky at all—
    So I have reached this nadir, have I?

The innocence of my child!
She believes that writing must be done
Only on manuscript paper.

> Somehow I have managed to pass this month safely.
> I have no more desire
> At the end of the month.

I used to tell lies,
I easily told lies—
I sweat at the thought of it.

> Reading old letters!
> Even from that fellow
> I was intimate with five years ago.

See,
Even that fellow has achieved a child.
So thinking, I go to bed consoled.

> "Ishikawa is a poor fellow."
> So telling myself,
> I try to sympathize with myself.

Pushing a door,
The patient stepped
Into an immeasurably long corridor.

>By the doctor's words,
>   "Don't you want to live, then?"
>   I was hushed.

I talked to him, but there was no response.
When I watched him closer,
The patient next to me was crying.

>One of the consolations on a fine day:
>I lean over a hospital window
>And smoke a cigarette.

The bustle in a room late at night—
Suspecting that somebody has died,
I hold my breath.

>On some days,
>The nurse's hand taking my pulse is warm,
>And on other days it is cold and stiff.

On the first night in the hospital
I fell asleep quickly—
Oh, how insensitive!

> That child:
> He, somehow, regarded himself
> As great.

At dawn, soaked in perspiration,
Torpid from uneasy slumber,
Alas, I am not fully awake!

> Leaning against the hospital window,
> I see various people
> Walking in good health.

Fearing my thoughts would be heard,
I quickly drew my chest back
From the stethoscope.

> On the other hand, I could secretly hope
> That I will grow sick enough
> To warrant a nurse's all-night vigil.

In the hospital
I return to my true self
Who longs for my wife and children.

> I decided not to tell a lie—
> This means that this morning
> I have told another lie.

For some reason
I felt myself to be a lump of lies,
And I closed my eyes.

> The inclination
> To pretend to be innocent
> After committing a very evil deed.

"Now, sleep quietly,"
    As if to a child,
    The doctor told me.

> On evenings when I cannot sleep,
> With a glint in my eyes under an ice-water bag,
>   I hate other people.

    Oh, the doctor is late!
Placing my hand on my painful chest
I close my eyes tight.

        I don't see anything
        Except the expression of the doctor
            On days when my chest aches so.

Today, for some reason,
    Many times
    I wished to own a gold watch.

        About the book I wish to publish someday,
        And about its cover,
            I talk to my wife.

Rejoicing over the color of the fresh salad,
    I took my chopsticks
And looked at it, but . . .

        What a shame to yell at my child.
            Wife,
            Don't blame my high fever.

I wondered
If fate had overtaken me—
Waking up at night under a heavy quilt.

Despite awareness of my thirst,
Today it is tiresome
To have to reach for an apple.

I have just heard a cuckoo in my dream.
It is sad
To have forgotten the cuckoos.

Five years after I left home,
In my sickness
I heard a cuckoo in my dream.

On a Japanese-cypress treetop,
Near the temple in my hometown,
A cuckoo bird came and cried.

The long corridor of that hospital—
I once wished
To reach its end.

    Pitiable
Are my skinny hands.
They no longer can close tight.

        I think
            Of the deep and remote cause of my illness;
            I think of it with my eyes closed.

Interestingly,
    There is a wish not to recover from my illness.
Where did that come from?

        I wished I had a new body
            As I rubbed the scar
            From the operation.

A long illness—
    The slight pleasure of forgetting
To take my medicine.

        This is the day
            When the Russian name, Borodin,
            Keeps coming to my mind.

The strangers who walk up to me, I am not sure when,
    Who hold my hand
And who leave me again.

        My friends and my wife seem to feel sad
        Since I never cease talking about revolutions
            Though in sickbed.

The terrorists' lamentable mind,
I had thought it far from mine—
    There are days when it comes close to mine.

        Today again, there is a pain in my chest.
            If I die,
            I will die in my hometown.

How many times
    Did I have to experience this!
Now I let fate decide my life.

        I happened to think:
            I can easily live on 8 cents a day
            In my home country.

Sick in bed for four months—
> The pleasant memory of the different medicines
> Which were changed from time to time.

> Sick in bed for four months—
>> The sorrow of seeing, in the meantime,
>> The noticeable increase in my child's stature.

What is this depression
That grows in my mind daily
> When I see my healthy child?

> I made my child sit beside my pillow.
> When I stared at her,
>> She ran away.

While I was considering my child to be
> A lot of nuisance,
She grew up to be five years old.

> Don't become like your father,
>> Don't become like your father's father—
> This is your father's wish, my child.

The five-year-old child:
    She has learned to say
    Words like *worker, revolution,* etc.

        Sometimes
        I praise the child who sings children's songs
            At the top of her voice.

    I wonder what she thought—
Leaving her toy, quietly,
My child came and sat beside me.

        Forgetting the time to get some sweets,
            From the second floor
        My child watches the city street.

Do you ask me, my wife,
    To explain my thoughts
About the days when we stared at the tatami-mats?

           My mother scolded me for the first time in many
                years
        For having forgotten to take my pills—
        How nice!

How undependable I am!
    On the days when I have a high temperature
And when my heart becomes like a meek animal.

        I took a pen
       Just to write:
      "The morning with some fresh flowers in my vase."

Today, my wife
Acts like a loose woman—
    I stare at a dahlia.

      As an event in his life in a certain town,
        A fellow told me of his love affair—
      The disappointment of finding lies mixed in his story.

For the first time in many years,
    I laughed aloud
At the sight of a fly rubbing its hands.

      The sorrow on days when I have a pain in my chest—
        Like a fragrant cigarette,
        It is hard to give up.

Myself of just a little while ago seems dear to me
    Who wished
    To raise a little fuss.

    To my five-year-old child
    I gave a Russian name, "Sonya," for no particular reason,
        And enjoyed calling it.

Placing myself
In the middle of an insoluble quarrel,
    I resent myself again.

    If we buy a cat,
    The cat will soon become the cause of our fights.
        Oh, my lamentable home!

"Would you send me to a boarding house,
Alone?"
    I almost said so again today.

    One day, momentarily, I forgot my illness
    And mimicked a cow's lowing
        During my family's absence.

Pitiable is my father!
    Because he is bored with the newspaper,
    He plays with some ants in the garden.

        I, the only son,
        Have grown up as I am—
            My parents must lament it.

My mother prays for my peace
Even by giving up her tea.
    I wonder what is upsetting her today.

        Suddenly today, I feel like playing with the children
            in the neighborhood.
        Though I call them, they do not come—
            I feel glum.

I haven't recovered,
Or died.
    Only my mind grows vehement this July and August.

        Oh, the consolation money-order from my
            friend—
        It arrived on the morning
        When I went short of medicine.

As I scolded my child,
She cried and went to bed.
    I touch her face sleeping with her mouth slightly open.

    Instinctively,
    I got up feeling my lung shrinking—
        On the morning close to autumn.

The autumn is near!
    The warmth of the lightbulb
Feels pleasant to my fingers.

    Beside my sleeping child
    I place a doll I just bought,
        And I rejoice.

When I say that Christ is a man,
    My sister's eyes
Show sorrow and pity.

    I have my pillow placed on the front porch.
        For the first time in a long while
        I enjoy the evening sky.

A white dog passed outside our garden:
    Turning around,
I beg my wife to keep the dog.

No Title (2)

1

Red! Red!
How much the color red
Makes this world gay!

2

Flowers, women, flags,
And blood!
Sunset in a desert,
The wave floating on the sea after a battle.

3

"Oh, can there be anything more lamentable than this?"
Having nothing better to do,
I just said this to myself
With strong intonation,
And I tried to conjure up the sad feeling
In my memory.
A yawn!

Shall I linger a little while yet and die?
There is no other alternative but to die!

4

Calmness!
There is no echo
In each nook and valley of my mind.
Wishing to hear something,
I make myself all ears

And scrutinize my state of mind.
Soon the memory of that woman arises.
"Let's go, yes, let's," I get dressed,
"To exchange lies."

5
Do you want me to say something?
Do you want me to laugh?
All right, all right, I know it—
Love is an exchange of flattery.
A pitiable woman!

Just a moment,
Just for awhile.
I cannot, I cannot laugh just yet.
I have a bad habit.

In a Wagon

No flower is blooming, but it is raining;
The young traveler in the wagon
Is myself.
Do not condemn my crying:
You, girls from Hakodate,
You, old people smoking cigarettes.
Courteous fellow-passengers,
Do not reproach me for crying.
Woman in poor clothes
With frost on your shaggy hair
And deep wrinkles in your gaunt face,
You graciously sit next to me.
At closer look
Your face resembles
That of my lonely mother in my home country.
Your unstarched, faded robe
Is like hers, too.
Your ripped sleeves as well are like hers.
You bring me back to my mother,
Misting my eyes.
Do not reproach me for crying,
Courteous fellow-passengers.

An Afternoon in My Study

I do not like the women of this country.

A foreign book I had been reading—
The rough texture of its pages
Does not readily absorb
The wine I spilt on them by accident.

I do not like the women of this country.

Home

This morning when I opened my eyes
I longed for a place to call my home.
I thought much about it while washing my face.
Returning home after a day's work,
As I sipped some tea and smoked a cigarette after supper,
The purple smoke reminded me of my dear past.
I sadly thought about "home"—
Sadly and in desolation.

Located not far from a railroad track,
I would choose the house at the end of a comfortable village.
A simple structure in a Western style:
Neither tall nor decorous,
With a wide staircase, a balcony, and a well-lit study…
And then, a chair pleasant to sit in.

I have thought many times about this house in the last few years.
Comparing the different arrangements of the rooms
According to the different times of the planning.
As I see the whiteness of my lampshade,
The pleasure of living in this house swarms in my imagination.
When I turn to the corner where my wife nurses her crying baby,
My lips curl up to smile in happiness.

In the meantime, the garden will be wide enough to let the wild weeds grow.
The joy of the summer shower falling on each leaf with a sound!
Also, in a corner, I will plant an enormous tree,
And I will place a white chair at its trunk.
On dry days, I will go out there
And will smoke those thick, tasty Egyptian cigarettes
As I cut open the pages of the new books
Sent by the Maruzen bookstore every week.
I shall doze till supper is announced,
And I will tell various stories to the country children
Who listen to me with their round eyes wide open …

But how sad,
I have parted from my younger days, heaven knows exactly when,
And I became weary of my everyday urban life.
But how sad,
I knew from the beginning that it is all vain
To have that dear and everlasting thought,
To say nothing of the many hopes unfulfilled so far.
With the gaze of my younger days when I was secretly in love,
Without telling my wife, I stare at the white lampshade
And, quietly but earnestly, go on daydreaming privately.

www.ingramcontent.com/pod-product-compliance
Lightning Source LLC
Chambersburg PA
CBHW031137090426
42738CB00008B/1116